The Gift

Clare Gill

ISBN:9798870059693

DEDICATION

This book is dedicated to Pam and Terry. Without you, it would not exist. Thank you for giving me the impetus to publish this collection. I am so grateful for your unwavering loyalty and support.

CONTENTS

ACKNOWLEDGMENTS

Thanks must go to Terry and Pam for their instigation of the publishing process which would otherwise remain dormant! Thanks also to Mark, for his love and support during what has been a particularly difficult few months. There would be no book without him. Thank you also to my family and friends who pick me up on a regular basis. And to Obi, my furry companion and the inspiration for many of my poems.

1 A BOY AND A DOG

A dog and a boy

A relationship formed

Which brings so much joy

The boy finds life hard

Prefers to be on his own

People don't understand

Even now that he's grown

The dog doesn't talk

Or torment the boy

He just looks into his eyes

Or brings him a toy

But that is enough

For them to be friends

The boy trusts the dog

Their love transcends

When times are tough

For the boy or his dog

They have each other

A unique analogue

A boy and a dog

A dog and a boy

A relationship formed

No one can destroy

2 FEELING LUCKY?

Are some people lucky

And some people not?

Or is everyone's luck

Taken from the pot?

Do you have lucky charms?

Or things that you wear?

When you need luck on your side

Do you even care?

A four leafed clover

Or a rabbit's foot?

Or perhaps a cat

Who's as black as soot?

Do you walk under ladders?

Collect pennies you find?

Step on cracks in the pavement?

Or is it all in your mind?

Does a broken mirror

Mean bad luck for years?

Do you knock on wood

To allay your fears?

Luck is created

And not engineered

So cross your fingers

You've nothing to fear!

3 CANOPHILIA

The eyes of a dog

Connected to your soul

Pull on your heartstrings

Make your life whole

You are his life

As he becomes yours

Connected forever

The one he adores

Look into those eyes

And it's plain to see

The love he has for you

Always will be

He depends on you

For every little thing

But in return

Loyalty unwavering

You are his world

His day and his night

Connected forever

A beautiful sight

4 BEFORE GOOGLE

What did parents do

When kids asked a difficult question or two ?

Before Google

When homework was hard

Out would come the library card

Before Google

When answers were needed

We all had a set of children's encyclopaedias

Before Google

When reading was a thing

We'd do our own research or give friends a ring

Before Google

Who did you believe?

Who gave you the knowledge so you could achieve?

Before Google

When I was a child

Life without technology, simply beguiled

5 CURIOSITY

How deep is the ocean?

Why is the sky blue?

Was it really Thomas Crapper

Who invented the loo?

How happy is Larry?

How far away is the sun?

How fast is a bullet

When it's shot from a gun?

Do cats have nine lives?

How cold is snow?

When you lose your voice

Where does it go?

Why is water wet?

How does the earth spin?

In a battle of wits

How do you win?

What colour is air?

Do stairs go up or down?

Is an upside down smile

Really a frown?

Can a leopard change it's spots?

How do clouds stay in the sky?

Why is it that some birds

Have wings but can't fly?

Can a heart really break?

Do soulmates exist?

Is anything possible

If you persist?

Can you solve the puzzle?

Look for the clue

Curiosity will aid you

In all that you do

6 TOAST

There's nothing more comforting

Than a slice of hot toast

Spread thickly with butter

When you need it the most

On a busy shift at work

When there's no time to rest

A single slice of toast

Is simply the best

Hot toast or cold

White bread or brown

Can make such a difference

When you're feeling down

My favourite toast

I share with you

No one can refuse

Toast made for two

It doesn't matter

What spread you choose

But a slice of toast

Can help to combat the blues

There is a reason why

Toast is known as comfort food

Eaten with cheese or beans

It's incredibly good

Toast

7 JUST SHUT UP!!

The tick of a clock

Or a dripping tap

Nails on a blackboard

A loud thunderclap

A noisy eater

Blowing your nose

Grinding teeth

Popping bubblewrap rows

Slurping a drink

A screaming kid

Incessant snoring

God forbid!

A mobile phone pinging

A fork on a plate

Any type of alarm

Or a creaking gate

Rustling wrappers

Biting nails

Barking dogs

Loud, howling gales

Burping or farting

Or someone throws up

Squeaking polystyrene

A spoon in a cup

Noisy breathing

Yawning too

Which of these

Would annoy you?!

8 THE PHOTOGRAPH

A moment in time

Captured forever

Memories made

Of time spent together

Happiness, sadness

Longing, content

Lost in a moment

Of time quickly spent

Loved ones remembered

Long after they've gone

Treasured pictures remind us

Of things we have done

Old photo albums

Are all we have left

Emotions tangible

When we are bereft

Sepia tones

Or black and white

THE GIFT

Blurry old Polaroids

Too dull or too bright

Corners bent over

Creases obscure

Handwritten notations

Too faint to be sure

Memories recorded

Lest you forget

People and places

A once much-loved pet

Take all the pictures

To treasure or share

A lifetime remembered

Emotions laid bare

9 YOU FIND SOMETHING FUNNY

When it's really not

And you're already laughing

Punchline long forgot

Your audience waiting

To share the joke

But you're laughing so hard

Only tears do evoke

Now everyone laughs

At the mere sight of you

Speech no longer possible

For a minute or two

Sides aching, chests hurting

Tears streaming down cheeks

In anticipation

Waiting for you to speak

As you reach the conclusion

Of your humorous tale

Hysteria has set in

Sensibilities fail

Gasping and laughing

We reach the punchline

Explosions of laughter

A moment divine

For the rest of the day

And for some time to come

You relive this moment

To stop you feeling glum

Randomly laughing

Incites curious stares

Questioning your sanity

But you don't really care

'Are you OK?'

'Yes, I'm fine thank you.'

'Do you want to share the joke?'

'No I don't think I do!

10 CHILD OF THE 70'S

My childhood was so different

From the one my children know

So many happy memories

From 50 years ago

Warm milk in little bottles

Milk monitors and straws

Ringing the bell at playtime

Spending all your time outdoors

French skipping and British Bulldog

A whole day in the park

Building dens and lighting fires

Going home when it got dark

Playing Kerby and Range Rover

Riding bikes and water fights

The youth club and Roller Disco

Was where we spent our nights

We played out when it was raining

No one minded getting wet

The banana slide and roundabout

Too dangerous to forget!

We recorded the charts on a Sunday

Poised to miss the talking bits

You had to time it just right

So none of the songs were missed

Reading books by Enid Blyton

Watching The Walton's on TV

Games of Monopoly and Connect 4

How simple life could be

We played with Sindy and Action Man

And often Pippa too

I had a black baby and Tiny Tears

And a Golliwog or two

No one had a mobile phone

Or computer or games console

Phones had dials and party lines

The phone book was quite a tome

We spent pennies buying mix ups

10p bought a lot of sweets

A 99 from the ice cream van

Was one of my favourite treats

Half pennies still existed

We all had pen pals too

Everyone went to Sunday school

Just for something to do

Children took themselves to school

The school run was not a thing

We had so much more freedom

And all the joy that brings

Discipline was different

Teachers used a ruler, slipper or cane

Parents would clip their kids round the ears

When they were being a pain

I wish my children could enjoy

A childhood more like mine

Looking back on times gone by

Reminds me of a childhood sublime

11 THE GOOD LIFE

Are you a good person

With kindness in your heart?

Do you make the best of every day

From the very start?

Do you make good choices?

For the greater good

Do you think of others?

Or even consider that you should?

Are you a good wife and mum?

Do your family know you care?

Are you a good colleague?

Who's support cannot compare?

Are you a good friend?

Creating bonds that never break

Are you a good pet owner?

That's a love you can't mistake

Are you a good neighbour?

Can you be relied upon?

Are you a good driver?

Or have those lessons been undone?

Can you look back on your life

Without any regrets?

Are there changes you would make

If you haven't yet?

Small changes make a big difference

When employed with sincerity

It's not too late for you to make

Your life the best that it can be

12 THE CLEANER IS COMING

I'd better tidy up

Hide those spoons in the dishwasher

And that dirty cup

Pick up the wet towels

The washing basket is full

Put a load in the machine

Chores are so dull!

Put the rubbish in the bin

Then make the bed

A cleaner will help you!

Isn't that what they said?

Straighten the cushions

On the three piece suite

Fold up the blanket

You used to cover your feet

Flush all the toilets

And make sure they're clean

Take the hair out of the plug holes

Too grim to be seen

Tidy the shoes

In the cupboard they go

And any other rubbish

No one will know!

Open the curtains

Shake the door mat

Lock the garage door

No one needs to see that!

It doesn't look too bad now

As you dust the TV

I have a cleaner

She's a great help to me!

13 NEURODIVERSITY

Your view of the world

Is different to mine

But always and forever

You'll be my sunshine

You teach me so much

A new point of view

In your black and white world

Just you being you

You struggle so much

With the simplest of things

Every time you succeed

It pulls on my heartstrings

It took us so long

To understand you

Now you are excelling

In all that you do

You've finally found

Your place in the world

You are achieving so much

Your power unfurled

Such a sensitive soul

With so many quirks

Now we've established

How your mind works

Different is not less

No matter what others say

My beautiful boy

In every way

14 TEXTING YOUR DAD

Is a joy to behold

You wait with baited breath

As the message unfolds

First, several emojis

As he gets in his stride

Their meaning irrelevant

You're sensing his pride

He used an emoji!

Who knew that was a thing?!

In his day you just waited

For the telephone to ring

There was none of this texting

You picked up the phone

What happened to talking?

Are those days long gone?

He continues his message

You wait with baited breath

For his literal masterpiece

Akin to Shakespeare's Macbeth

But it's only a sentence

Perhaps even two

Explaining the emojis

Well you asked, didn't you?

So you reply in great detail

To his question to you

And get no response

You see he's logged off too!

His achievement is palpable

How happy he must be

Grinning from ear to ear

Self-congratulatory

So there you have it

When you text an old man

He may not reply

Even if he can

They like to keep you hanging

Wondering when they'll reply

Probably in a day or two

And then just to say 'bye'!

You imagine his frustration

Getting the 'damn thing' to send

And then he phones you anyway

Because it drives him round the bend

Dare you suggest Facebook

Or would Instagram be better?

Now he's down with technology

Quite the pacesetter!

15 MISERABLE MONDAY

Every shade of grey

Tireless Tuesday

No time to play

Wonderful Wednesday

Halfway through the week

Tedious Thursday

Excitement you seek

Fabulous Friday

Anticipates the weekend

Soporific Saturday

Relaxing to the end

Suddenly it's Sunday

And your week is done

In a flash it's all over

A new week has begun!

16 YOU CAN'T OVERSLEEP

So you set your alarm

The anticipation

Prevents you feeling calm

You check your alarm

To ensure it's set

Then you check it again

In case you forget

An early night

Is what you need

Plenty of sleep

And you will succeed

So you prepare

Things for the next day

Then when you wake

You can get on your way

Then you get into bed

For an early night

If you go to sleep now

It will be just right

Eight blissful hours

Of wonderful rest

So in the morning

You'll be at your best

You toss and you turn

But you can't go to sleep

You're getting agitated

Don't suggest counting sheep!

You have a quick drink

And go to the loo

Turn on your mood lighting

And oil diffuser too

You ask Alexa

For meditation for sleep

And you even consider

Counting those sheep!

Nothing is working

You're still wide awake

Now you'll only get 7 hours

For goodness sake!

You lie with your eyes closed

And empty your head

But sleep can't be achieved

Just by lying in bed

You look at the time

Your biggest regret

Six measly hours

Is all you will get

You turn on your side

Cover over your head

And then your other half

Decides to come to bed

He gets into bed

Ablutions complete

Turns on the TV

And puts cream on his feet

He notices your sigh

And begins to chat

Doesn't he realise

You'll get 5 hours, if that?!

You pretend to be sleeping

And wish that you were

As he begins snoring

Without a care

So now you are listening

To his every breath

The TV is blaring

You're planning his death

You yank on his pillow

A recently learned trick

The snoring abates

Is he taking the mick?!

I'm down to four hours!

Panic sets in

I need to sleep

There's no chance I'll win

Now he is coughing

An asthma attack

My oil diffuser

Is making him hack

Inhaler retrieved

From his office downstairs

What time is it now?

Nobody cares

You can't get comfy

The dog's in a state

He stands sniffing the air

Out by the garden gate

We're all back in bed

Normal breathing resumes

Oil diffuser switched off

We've aired out the room

By now it is freezing

And I'm wide awake

There's not much more of this

That I can take!

I look at the clock

How is it half past four?

I'm not going to bother

To try to sleep anymore

In the blink of an eye

When I've just gone to sleep

What is that awful noise?

Beep beep beep BEEEEEEEEP!!!

Oh whoop de doo!

It's time to awaken

A peaceful night

Desperately foresaken

17 PARENTING TEENAGERS

A whirlwind of hormones

And mess and smells

Learning a new language

No parallels

Freedom and love

Rebellion and hate

Success and celebration

Deciding their fate

Finding their place

In a tumultuous world

Future uncertain

Opportunity unfurled

Support and understanding

Unconditional love

Patience unbounded

And strength from above

Teach them self-belief

Effort is rewarded

And always be kind

Friendship afforded

Follow your heart

And make mistakes

Learning from them

Is all it takes

Teenagers test you

Make you question and doubt

But you know you've succeeded

When they finally move out!

18 HAVING A BABY

Is such a wonderful thing

Completing your family

So much joy they will bring

The first one is easy

But you don't realise

As you stress about milestones

There's no compromise

Number two comes along

By now you're a pro

But this kid is different

So much you don't know

But you muddle through

Two kids in the bag

Parenting is easy

But you're not one to brag

Two kids have survived

Your slack parenting

Both decent humans

Despite everything

Then in a crazy moment

A third kid appears

What could possibly go wrong?

The sum of all your fears?

This kid will test you

To your limits and more

You cannot rely on

What worked before

It will take a long time

To get to know him

And you'll learn so much

You can't act on a whim

Third children teach you

How to truly parent

To live in his world

And never relent

Families are messy

But bring so much joy

The effort is worth it

Just look at my boys!!

19 A JUMBLE OF LETTERS

A few mismatched words

Mixed up thoughts in your head

The picture is blurred

No clear ideas

Nothing comes to mind

You try different tactics

In a hope you might find

A hint of a spark

Of a glimpse of something

The tiniest flicker

So much hope it will bring

And then from that spark

The ideas flow

The words tumble out

Filling row by row

Before you know it

You've written a verse

A verse of a poem

THE GIFT

You did not rehearse

Verse follows verse

Until you have some prose

It's amazing how easy

It is to compose

So that's how you do it

When your stuck for a theme

Just give it a moment

It's easier than it seems

20 PATTERNS OF LIFE

Raindrops mark their course

On the window pane

Streaks across the sky

Of a holidaying plane

Frozen dew drops held

On a spider's web

Waves upon the sand

When the tide is on the ebb

Footprints in the earth

I wonder what led them here?

Lines upon your face

Your story year on year

Children walking to school

An army heading to war

The colourful array

Of pebbles on the shore

Red bricks lined up in rows

Every wall the same

THE GIFT

Pixels on the screen

Of a computer game

Stars form constellations

In the sky at night

Shadows created on the ground

When the sun is bright

Colourful fruit and vegetables

On a market stall

Flowers wild and beautiful

Can be enjoyed by all

A double helix of DNA

Unique to only you

Feathers of a peacock

A lovely shade of blue

Words upon a page

Feelings chronicled

Oceans and continents

Our amazing world!

21 WHEN TIMES ARE HARD

And you are sad

Think of the good days

You have had

Remember things

That made you smile

Even if you haven't

For a while

Put on some music

To lift you up

Have a drink

In your favourite cup

Eat something nice

Like homemade cake

Watch TV

Or just have a break

Talk to friends

Who really care

The ones you know

Will always be there

Walk the dog

Or stroke the cat

Speak to a stranger

It’s good to chat

Whatever you do

Don’t mope about

It’s better to share

Of that there’s no doubt

22 THERE'S NOTHING NICER THAN A CUP OF TEA

Freshly brewed, simplicity

A long-lasting brew to start the day

Or a hastily snatched mug along the way

Tea provides a welcome break

When there's not much more that you can take

A mutual cuppa shared with friends

Interspersed chatter that never ends

When people visit, we offer them tea

The epitome of friendly

Tea is routine, it punctuates the day

Creating routine along the way

Tea is for waking and taking to bed

Moments of clarity, when everything's been said

Tea cheers you up when you're feeling low

Decisions made when you just don't know

Tea itself can bring relief

The perfect antidote for grief

At half past ten or five to three

It's always the perfect time for tea

Brewed in mug or in a pot

As long as it is nice and hot

A splash of milk or drink it black

On its own or with a snack

Tea is a British constitution

Ask anyone, tea is the solution!

23 BE KIND

Whatever the weather

Whatever the day

Be generous of thought

In all that you say

Whatever your feelings

Whatever your mood

Focus on the positives

And all that is good

Whatever your worries

Whatever your strife

Don't take more than you give

Making your way through life

Whatever your gripe

Whatever your groan

You bring people down

If all you do is moan

Whatever you think

Whatever you do

Reflect for a moment

On how others see you

Whatever your hopes

Whatever your dreams

Never give up

It's easier than it seems

Whatever your motive

Whatever inspires

Don't walk over others

When your heart desires

Whatever you want

Whatever you need

If you are kind to others

You'll always succeed

24 THE SNACK

You've eaten your meal

And watched some TV

Now you are bored

And convinced you're hungry

Your rational mind

Knows that can't be true

Your stomach won't be silenced

No matter what you do

You need a snack

Just something sweet

Nothing substantial

A morsel, a treat

You look in the fridge

Nothing satisfies

There's just some cheese

And an ancient pork pie

Hope ignited

By a chocolate roll

But the packet is empty

The proverbial black hole

You continue your search

Frustration abounds

There must be a snack

Just waiting to be found

You check all the cupboards

Not once, but twice

You even search your work bag

But don't find anything nice

You ask your husband

To locate his hidden stash

He professes not to have one

But offers me cash

Too lazy to go out

Disappointed by greed

I must find a snack

I will succeed

My search is fruitless

But I'm not beaten yet

Peanut butter and a spoon

The best snack you can get!!

25 I SENT YOU A MESSAGE

Because I care

I sent you a message

Because I can't be there

I sent you a message

I know it's not the same

I sent you a message

So you will know I came

I sent you a message

Words from the heart

I sent you a message

Forced to be apart

I sent you a message

Expressing how I feel

I sent you a message

The sentiments were real

I sent you a message

Text is not the same as a call

I sent you a message

You've not replied at all...

26 CARE

Care is Compassion

In all that you do

Care is Patience

Practiced by too few

Care is Time

No matter how long it takes

Care is Attention

And the difference that makes

Care is Advocating

For the best thing for you

Care is Listening

You have a voice too

Care is Concern

For your health and well-being

Care is Supporting

All parties agreeing

Care is Love

Unspoken yet felt

Care is Understanding

The cards you've been dealt

Care is Acknowledging

When you're in pain

Care is Devotion

Feelings are plain

Care is beautiful

A reason to be proud

Care is Fulfilling

Determination avowed

Care is Simple

It's just what you do

Care is Enduring

Believing in you

Care is Hope

Never giving in

Care is a Battle

You sometimes can't win

27 THE WAITING GAME

Deafening in your ear

Seconds pass so slowly

When you're waiting to hear

Nights are long

Sleep escapes you

Thoughts prevent rest

No matter what you do

The routine of the day

Is your marker of time

You're watching life happen

A complex paradigm

Everyone else

Going about their day

Unaware of the game

You are forced to play

The hustle and bustle

Distracts you somewhat

You're on autopilot

A dysfunctional robot

You long for resolution

This game has to end

The outcome is certain

Feelings transcend

But in the meantime

You continue to wait

Trapped in a bubble

Playing a game that you hate

28 LOVE IS A LOOK

A connection profound

Love is a touch

Tenderness abounds

Love is a feeling

Devotion to you

Love is a gesture

Nothing to construe

Love is understanding

Unspoken bonds

Love is trust

Truth corresponds

Love is respect

Your feelings matter

Love is unpredictable

Not presented on a platter

Love is hopeful

A reason to go on

Love is inevitable

Conclusion foregone

Love is natural

Effortless and unforced

Love is reciprocated

Mutual feelings endorsed

Love is imperfection

Perfection is flawed

Love is vulnerability

Protected and adored

Love is enduring

Eternal faithfulness

Love is honesty

Nothing to confess

Love is kindness

No exception

Love is silence

Peaceful perception

Love is complete

No need to explain

Love is everlasting

Forever sustained

I love you x

29 FRIENDS

My friends are:

The light to my dark

The silence to my bark

The happy to my sad

The good to my bad

The laughter to my tears

The calm to my fears

The brightness to my dull

The efficacious to my null

The respect to my disdain

The pleasure to my pain

The early to my late

The love to my hate

The joy to my doom

The light to my gloom

The less to my more

The peace to my war

The owt to my nowt

The assurance to my doubt

The short to my tall

The rise to my fall

The black to my white

The day to my night

The hot to my cold

The young to my old

The strong to my weak

The hope to my bleak

My friends are EVERYTHING

30 THANK GOODNESS FOR YOU

A cold wet nose

Those puppy dog eyes

A wagging tail

Nothing defies

That trusting stare

Devout loyalty

Unconditional love

For an eternity

A proffered paw

A tilted head

Unwavering attention

To every word you've said

A comforting nudge

When you feel sad

Silent comprehension

Your furry comrade

Your personal trainer

Your partner in crime

Your constant companion

Your keeper of time

Always ready to listen

A sharer of woe

He'll take any praise

You're prepared to bestow

He hangs on every word

He's your very best friend

Bonded forever

Together to the end

31 HAPPY VALENTINE'S DAY!

A tradition of romance

Cards and flowers

A tentative glance

A secret admirer

Or long-declared love

Hit with Cupid's arrow

Symbolised by a dove

Gifts for the occasion

Bought by anxious men

Dates planned in advance

Not to be forgotten

But if you love someone

Truly, madly, deeply…

You tell them every single day

You love them completely

You don't wait for one day

When the world says you should

Express your love for another

To make you feel good

My husband knows that I love him

With every breath that I take

He is my soulmate

A bond no one can break

He knows that I love him

When he catches my eye

The way he looks at me

A love no man can deny

He knows when he holds me

And I can hear his heartbeat

In that single moment

He makes me complete

He knows when his hand

Accidentally brushes mine

I still get a tingle

All the way down my spine

I know that he loves me

When he squeezes my hand

Silent reassurances

He understands

I know that he loves me

When he strokes my hair

His tender embrace

Confirmation he cares

I know that he loves me

When he champions me

His pride is evident

For all to see

I know that he loves me

The world knows it too

Every beat of our hearts

Saying I love you ♥

32 THE DOG WALK

When we left the house

The sky was blue

Perfect for a dog walk

Just me and you

We set off

On our familiar route

Puddles no problem

I'd donned wellington boots

The sun shining brightly

As we ambled along

Peace interrupted

By only birdsong

We get to the place

Where the dog can run free

As he circumnavigates

Me, full of glee

His ears are flapping

His eyes are bright

He circles me again

You can sense his delight

All of a sudden

He slams into me

As I lose my balance

He's laughing at me!

Then as I'm distracted

By a noise far away

I lose sight of the dog

As he runs off to play

I look up at the sky

As black clouds block the sun

I must locate the dog

And put an end to his fun

It's going to rain

It's time to head back

I'm not prepared for a storm

An umbrella I lack

I call the dog's name

And pretend to leave

The dog isn’t fooled

He’s not so naive

Eventually he appears

And I tether him again

Just as the heavens open

It’s starting to rain

The dog looks peculiar

His mouth open wide

We stop to take a look

There’s something inside

It looks like a bone

But he won’t let me see

Now it’s pouring down

So I just leave him be

We make our way home

Me and my idiot dog

Howling wind and pouring rain

It’s become a hard slog

He looks pretty funny

With his mouth open wide

Carrying his prize

It's not easy to hide

By the time we get home

We're both soaked to the skin

What was I thinking?!

You can sense my chagrin

33 MOMENTS

Life is a series of moments

Connected intricately

Moments you remember

Create your life story

Interwoven with others

Are moments that you share

But some moments are yours alone

Your story cannot compare

You savour every moment

As it is unique to you

As time goes by and memories fade

These moments are all too few

At your story's conclusion

These moments still remain

In the form of memories

An eternal daisy chain

The memories you leave begot

By the person you are

Loved ones hold dear those moments

Cherished from afar

34 THERE'S STORMY WEATHER HERE TODAY

First Dudley, then Eunice came to play

Now we hear Franklin's on his way

There's stormy weather here today

There's stormy weather here today

The wind is strong and trees will sway

There is no sun, the sky is grey

There's stormy weather here today

There's stormy weather here today

In the house I'd like to stay

I watch the rain from my doorway

There's stormy weather here today

There's stormy weather here today

The gales have blown the bins away

So many things have gone astray

There's stormy weather here today

There's stormy weather here today

It's set to last, the weathermen say

Even the dog won't go out to play

There's stormy weather here today

There's stormy weather here today

A good excuse for a lazy Sunday

I don't need an excuse, I have to say!

There's stormy weather here today

35 THE HUG

Warm

Soft

Strong,

Tight

Loving

Long,

Affectionate

Friendly

Embrace,

Comfortable

Bear

Face to face,

Romantic

Eternal

Cuddle,

Tentative

Endearing

Huddle,

Welcome

Cherished

Returned,

Hopeful

Compassion

Earned,

Tender

Sensitive

Kind,

Close

Powerful

Entwined

36 GRIEF

At dawn, when we wake

We think of you

When thoughts rob us of sleep

We think of you too

You should be here

But you have gone

Constant reminders

Of a life undone

Your room, untouched

Remains the same

As the day you left

There is no claim

Your clothes lie folded

In a pile

Too soon to dispose of

In denial

Food uneaten

Where it was left

Last touched by you

Now bereft

Flowers fading

Drooping as they wilt

The vase bears your fingerprints

Memories inbuilt

The things you used

Everyday

Now hold only sentiment

Can't be thrown away

The chair where you sat

Vacant emptiness

Life goes on

Nevertheless

Missing you

And all you stood for

A mother's love

For ever more

A life cut short

Suddenly gone

Rest in peace

Never alone

Always in our thoughts

And in our heart

Bonds unbroken

Never apart

Our tears will fall

Memories of you

We'll never forget

Feelings so true

37 THE PASSWORD

You must think of a password

You will not forget

Something you'll remember

And haven't used yet

The name of your dog

A memorable date

The address of your first house

Something you hate

The names of your children

All merged together

Your favourite holiday

Or favourite weather

Your favourite band

Or favourite food

Whatever you choose

You'd better make it good

Between 8 and 12 characters

A capital or two

Maybe a number

Something unique to you

You try all the usual

Easy to bring to mind

But apparently they're 'weak'

And really not refined

The suggestions they make

Ridiculous at best!

Unless learning nonsense

Is the aim of your quest?!

Random numbers and letters

Special characters too

You'll never remember it

Unless you write it down too

So you carefully write down

Usernames and passwords

So you don't forget

Defiantly undeterred

Conveniently located

In a dedicated notebook

Access to everything

All it takes is a quick look

But you have your new password

That didn't take long

Written in a notebook

What could possibly go wrong?!

38 SHREDDING MEMORIES

We've upgraded the shredder

It's tougher you see

18 sheets at a time

It should be easy

Boxes of paperwork

Taking up space

For years we have kept it all

Stored 'just in case'

It's time to get rid of it

Not looked at for years

And now resident mice

Are increasing my fears

I hope it's just bank statements

And old uni stuff

Bills and old paperwork

And a fair amount of fluff

As I begin shredding it

Some treasures I find

Forgotten photographs

Somehow left behind

Cards made by my children

When they were small

Pictures and memories

I want to keep them all

Then I find a leaflet

For the place I gave birth

That was 18 years ago

What else will I unearth?

My postnatal records

For baby number 2

Such a fascinating read

Considering the job I now do

Lost in my memories

Of a previous life

When my children were tiny

And I was a brand new wife

Shredding now forgotten

These boxes hold so much more

Than old bills and cheque book stubs

They hold memories I adore

39 PANCAKES

Batter mixed

Pancakes tossed

Carefully

So none are lost

Eaten hot

Taken from the pile

Can't be beaten

By a mile

A squeeze of lemon

Will taste good

A sprinkle of sugar

To sweeten the mood

Chocolate spread

A scoop of ice cream

A handful of berries

Or something more extreme?

You can't just have one

How many will it be?

Until you feel sick?

Or just two or three?

Happy Shrove Tuesday

Whatever you do

Have a pancake

It will make you smile too

40 THE DECISION

At times in your life

You've decisions to make

Important decisions

Not just, shall you have cake?!

Decisions affect

More than just you

So many life choices

What will you do?

Will you have a life partner?

Where will you live?

How many children?

If hurt, will you forgive?

What will your job be?

Will you have a career?

Do you have a good social life?

Or do you live in fear?

Do you plan for the future?

Do you have good health?

Do you have life goals?

Beyond more than wealth?

Are decisions made for you?

Do you feel in control?

Are you truly happy?

In your heart and your soul?

Don’t do things on impulse

Give some careful thought

And the decision you make

Will be the one that you ought

It’s never easy

Life choices are hard

Always choose what makes you happy

It reaps its own reward

41 WORLD BOOK DAY

For one day in March

Every year

World Book Day

Fills parents with fear

Costumes required

Representing favourite books

It has to be good

Or you'll get funny looks

Favourite characters

Must be brought to life

Each year more intricate

Causing more strife

One rule we had

For World Book Day

Was they must read the book

Or they don't get a say

I made my boys costumes

Not bought from a shop

Never straightforward

Kept me on the hop

Now my boys have grown up

World Book Day's not a thing

I miss making costumes

And the joy that it brings

I don't miss the stress

Of the night before

Creating the costume

Was always a chore

But when it was done

Grinning from ear to ear

Happy World Book Day

For another year!

42 THE HAIR DYE

My favourite shade

Is red, by far

But the upkeep is terrible

I buy it in a jar

The persistent greys

Soon make their presence known

It doesn't take long

My hair has barely grown

So out comes the dye

It's a regular chore

To keep the red glorious

Like it was before

The process itself

Should be simple, I know

But it's harder each time

As I let my hair grow

The scene in my bathroom

Is like a blood bath

I even surprise myself

At the aftermath

Red dye gets everywhere

And stains everything

Particularly walls

And definitely skin

But the results are worth it

Now my hair is dyed

Back to lush red

No more need to hide!

43 THE MICE

There are mice in the garage

They've gorged on dog food

A hole in the bag

Dog food must taste good

Droppings everywhere

They get into everything

They've nibbled some paperwork

And eaten some string

They've even made a nest

In Joe's roller boot

All cosy and fluffy

Surrounded by loot

No bag left unturned

As contents are spilled

No care for our stuff

Mice are really quite free-willed

So we cleared out the garage

Got rid of their bed

All food sources gone

They're in the loft now instead!!!

44 THE MICE: PART 2

We thought we'd eradicated the mice

Residing in our garage

But evidence to the contrary

Continued sabotage

They'd hidden themselves carefully

To avoid detection

Their cover blown accidentally

By a discarded confection

As their presence was realised

Incidentally

Damage to my jumper

I take personally!

The jumper was in my work bag

Ready for today

Good job I check the night before

Or imagine my dismay

Pulling that jumper out of my bag

After my shift at work

Holes aplenty, chewed fibres

I'd have gone berserk

So now the mice have to go

They've outstayed their welcome

The Pied Piper could help me out

As the resident cat is quite dumb

45 A RAINBOW OF SPRING FLOWERS

Red are the tulips

Love, perfect and deep

Orange ranunculus

Happiness you can keep

Yellow are daffodils

They symbolise spring

Green are the hellebores

Tranquility they bring

Blue are the bluebells

A symbol of humility

Indigo are anemones

Anticipation of what may be

Violet are violets

Bringing everlasting love

A rainbow of spring flowers

New beginnings hereof

46 THE THRILLER

There's a new thriller

On the TV

It's in four parts

Described as a 'must see'

So I watch the first part

As the story unfolds

Characters introduced

Plot lines remain untold

By the second episode

You think you've worked it out

But there's another twist

Now you're filled with doubt

Some questions are answered

In the third episode

But who dunnit's a mystery

Still to unfold

As the fourth episode airs

Your assumptions are proved wrong

Who would have guessed

It was him all along?

Then your mum sends a text

Asking what it was all about

She's watched the whole series

And can't work it out

Who was the bloke?

How did he die?

Who was the woman?

Was it all a lie?

By the time you've explained

And it's still clear as mud

The thriller you watched

No longer seems so good

But after more questions

You've worked it out

She's watched a different series

Of that there's no doubt

No wonder her questions

Didn't make sense

Watching two different programmes

The confusion was immense!

47 THE REALITY OF PARKINSON'S

I worked all weekend

Now I can hardly move

Staying in bed

Won't help things to improve

I haven't slept

Symptoms kept me awake

There is a limit

To how much you can take

My tremor is worse

But that aside

That is the symptom

I usually hide

The invisible symptoms

Give me so much more grief

Medication ineffective

There is no relief

Pain and stiffness

Causing misery

Fatigue and brain fog

All normal for me

But my brain has to work harder

Doing daily activities

So add in a job

And I’m on my knees

I’m not looking for sympathy

I don’t need people to care

It would make my life easier

If people were aware

My medication wears off

Several times a day

During those periods

I can’t keep symptoms at bay

Simple tasks become difficult

As I try hard to hide

Resurfacing symptoms

I cannot abide

I just need a moment

For medication to kick in

Parkinson's is my daily battle

I'm fighting so hard to win

48 A MOTHER'S LOVE

The love for a child

Cannot compare

Unconditional, timeless

Catches you unaware

You'd sacrifice your life

In a heartbeat

The love of a child

So perfect and sweet

In a single moment

They've captured your heart

You love them so deeply

Right from the start

Their love is unrivalled

Takes your breath away

How can you possibly

Love them more each day?

And with each child

That love simply grows

You cannot explain it

But a mother knows

The love for a child

Simple and true

No matter where life takes them

They will always love you

49 THE TEST

Life is a test

Of the person you are

Will you settle for less?

Or will you go far?

Do you have a life plan?

Or goals to achieve?

Can you choose your fate?

Do you believe?

You'd choose to be loved

Successful and happy

If the decision was yours

And choices were free

Difficult days

Still have a place

A way for us to learn

From the challenges we face

If you navigate the storms

And still manage to smile

The effort you make

Will be so worthwhile

No matter what

Life throws at you

Celebrate opportunities

Only too few

Chances to show

What makes you great

How you perform

Determines your fate

Some people are lucky

Challenges are few

Others rise to the challenge

In all that they do

Life isn't easy

It's not meant to be

The test will determine

Who you will be

50 FOR THE LOVE OF DOGS

Dog hair on the furniture

Dog hair on your clothes

Dog hair is a prerequisite

Every dog owner knows

Dog toys hidden in your bed

Dog toys on the stairs

Stuffing from those dog toys

Is strewn everywhere

Muddy paw prints on the door mat

Muddy paw prints on the floor

As quickly as you get rid of them

The dog's producing more

Barking at the doorbell

Barking to get you to play

Barking just because he can

And he's got a lot to say

Zoomies when he's excited

Zoomies when he's bored

Zoomies just because it's fun

Or when he feels ignored

Wagging his tail when he's happy

Wagging his tail to say hello

Half a wag when he's unsure

When he's scared the wag will go

Love for his favourite human

Loyalty to his family

Companionship and devotion

For an eternity

51 SPRINGTIME

The world is reawakening

Spring flowers are in bloom

A host of golden daffodils

And hyacinths perfume

Blossom decorates the trees

New leaves are in bud

New life is emerging

Just as it should

Hibernation over

Hedgehogs look for food

Dormice and bats awaken

Boxing hares up to no good

The return of the dawn chorus

Heralding the new day

The call of the cuckoo

As it leaves its eggs astray

Lambs gambolling in the fields

Swallows on the wing

Bluebells carpet woodland floors

As we celebrate Spring

52 THE WORRIER

A lot on your mind

Thoughts weigh heavily

Cannot be resolved

What will be, will be

And yet still you lose sleep

As you think things through

Mulling over options

What should you do?

You cannot decide

Ultimately fate will dictate

It doesn’t change the fact

You worry while you wait

And then the day comes

When all becomes clear

Was all the stress worth it?

Are things as bad as you fear?

Probably not!

You worry excessively

Worst case scenarios

My speciality

53 THE LOVE STORY

Boy meets girl

Girl meets boy

A bond created

No man can destroy

Hearts a flutter

When they first met

Overwhelmed by desire

Never to forget

A brief encounter

Ignites a flame

Passion or desire

They both feel the same

A smile or a touch

A lingering look

A relationship formed

On a chance they both took

Now decades later

Still very smitten

A lifetime together

Their love story written

54 THE EMPTY NEST

At first there are two of you

Building your nest

Small to begin with

There's time for the rest

Then there's a baby

And two becomes three

Your nest is still cosy

A brand new family

Baby number two

Puts a strain on the nest

You must build another

Before you can rest

The new nest is bigger

Room for babies to grow

You make it your home

Your own tiny chateau

Then out of the blue

Baby number three

Makes his appearance

Now this nest is too wee

So you find a new nest

Perfect for you all

The babies can grow

This nest isn't too small

Years go by

Children grow into men

They leave the nest

And don't come back again

They have their own lives

And their own families

You have an empty nest

And great memories

55 WHO ARE YOU?

When people look at you

Who do they see?

Do you get to choose

Who you want to be?

Do they see a mum

Or a daughter or wife?

Do they see the career

You've chosen for life?

Do they see the label

Life has chosen for you?

Which in no way reflects

What you want it to

Do they see a person

Dealt a tough hand?

Or do they just see the scars?

They don't understand

Do they see the illness

You try so hard to hide?

Choice taken away

You don’t get to decide

Do they see emotion

Happy or sad?

Defining your character

Though it drives you mad

You’re not any of those things

You are just you

Look below the surface

For an image that’s true

56 INSPIRE ME!

Who inspires you

Every day?

Is it the way they behave?

Or the things that they say?

Have they set their sights high?

What can you achieve?

Or is it simply a matter of

If you believe?

Do they have a great attitude?

Someone you admire

Generosity and kindness?

Qualities to aspire

Or are they just a nice person?

Humble and true

Making a difference

In all that they do

Who ever you choose

Whatever they do

Find someone worthy

To inspire you!

And in return

You too can inspire

Be a role model

So others aim higher

Be kind person

In all that you do

Then others will want

To be more like you

57 POETRY

Prose or a limerick

Written from the heart

It doesn't even have to rhyme

Your style sets you apart

It's a way to reflect

And say how you feel

Vent your frustrations

Emotions so real

Document your life

In a few lines of prose

Important events

Things no one else knows

Poetry is a great way

To express how you feel

Give it a try

You will see the appeal

You don't have to share it

You can write just for you

Just put pen to paper

And write a line or two

I write my poetry

Not just to share

Fundraising for Parkinson's UK

Because I care

If you enjoy my poems

Consider the effort it takes

A few pennies from you

And the difference that makes

The challenge is far from over

A quarter way through!

I'm committed to complete it

Grateful for support from you

58 THE BOILER

The boiler is broken

Timing is great

Temperatures plummet

I'm sure you can relate

No heating or hot water

Parts can't be found

You need an engineer

There's no one around

Your husband gets mad

The house is so cold

No one can shower

Can't be done, we're told

How long do they expect

Us to survive this?

No heat or hot water

They're taking the p***

Last time it was 3 weeks

Will they break their record?

Whatever it takes

Is already more than I can afford

I don't do cold showers

Strip washes aren't cool

Even the dog isn't impressed

He's nobody's fool!

Just fix the boiler

How hard can it be?

How long will it take?

The complaint is free!

59 THE HAIRCUT

You decide to cut your hair off

But it's Sunday today

No salons are open

There will be a delay

You have no hot water

Your boiler cannot be fixed

To compound a problem

That didn't really exist

So you boil the kettle

And come up with plan B

You'll just ask your husband

It will be easy!

You fill the sink with water

And try to wash your hair

Water is going everywhere

But you don't really care

You're on a mission

For a hair cut today

This is as good as it gets

It will be okay

Hair wrapped in a towel

Clippers and scissors in hand

You present yourself to your hubby

Who doesn’t understand

You get him up to speed

And reveal your plan

You don’t give him a choice

There’s no question of ‘can’

You tell him what to do

He’s off to a great start

Hair falls to the floor

But it’s looking quite smart

Then you remember

You should have sectioned it first

Does it really matter?

We’ll do it in reverse

So when thinks he finished

We start over again

This time with sections

He says I'm being a pain

He asks me to strip

A bit presumptuous I think

And then rubs me down

With a cold cloth from the sink

Not the usual technique

Of hairdressers I know

I think if it was

No one would go

After the wet cloth

He declares he is done

So I cut my own fringe

A big chunk is now gone

I'm sure it will be fine

When I've styled it like so

You'll never notice

No one will ever know

Salon Gill

The place to come

If you want a hair cut

And a wee bit of fun

Totally unqualified

Totally free

My kind of haircut

Salon Gill is for me!

60 THE SWAN

Beauty unrivalled

Majestic, untamed

Finest monochrome

Masterpiece framed

Snowy white plumage

Graceful and true

Defenders of faith

And loyalty too

Serenity personified

Partners for eternity

Glide through still waters

Such regality

Fiercely protective

Aggressively portrayed

Only when provoked

Distinctions must be made

A beautiful creature

Graceful and free

Symbolic of love

Forever shall be

61 THE SHOWER

No shower for a week

And not because I'm unclean

The boiler was broken

No engineer to be seen

We waited for a part

Then the part didn't fit

So we waited a bit longer

For an extra bit

Then we had all the parts

But needed an engineer

They don't work weekends

Well not around here

So today was the day

We had all waited for

A family of five

Who can't take any more

We're not being unreasonable

But strip washes aren't great

You can't get squeaky clean

Unless you can shower at mates

Then the neighbours get suspicious

When the whole family

Turn up where your mum's staying

In an air BnB

You have to take chances

And wash wherever you can

Anything to avoid

Boiling water in a pan

So I get home from work

After a very long day

We have hot water

Hip, hip hooray!!

I can't tell you how it felt

It was music to my ears

Just to wash properly

The best shower in years

But the saga's not over

We still have no heat

Another night of extra blankets

And fluffy socks on my feet

It was too much to ask

For heating to be fixed too

The engineer is returning

He thinks he knows what to do

I'll update you tomorrow

After he's been

For now I'm relishing

How it feels to be really clean!!

62 THE NEW KITCHEN

My lovely new kitchen

Is almost complete

Decorators booked

For the end of the week

We saved for a long time

To have the kitchen done

It seems an eternity

Since it was begun

It will be worth the wait

A kitchen I can use

Now and in the future

Despite that old Parkinson's ruse

However I have discovered

A kitchen shiny and new

Will create issues

For your husband, not you!

He can't resist cleaning

Many times a day

If there's a mark or a smear

He must wipe it away

And as for appliances

So many are new

A little bit tricky

When you don't know what to do

This is my life now

He sits in front of the hob

Adjusting the settings

I think he needs a new job!!

And then when he's satisfied

The pan won't boil over

He gets out the manual

And reads it cover to cover

There's no peace in my kitchen

My oasis of calm

The novelty had better wear off

Before I do him some harm!!

But I do love my kitchen

So much I can ignore

My special husband

And his unnecessary chore!

63 THE DRILL BRUSH

What an invention

A brush for a drill!

If anyone would try it

You might know, I will!

The cleaner's gone AWOL

So the house is a disgrace

From my 'to do' list

The shower is a task I must face

I hate cleaning the shower

It's such a horrible chore

All those tiny little tiles

And that annoying glass door

But here I was armed

With a brush and a drill

A variety of cleaning products

And not nearly enough will

I set to work, thinking

This would be easy

The drill brush and some bleach

Would do the job for me

Mark had assured me

There would be no spray

So dressed in my nightie

I made a start, no delay

I soon realised

Mark's assessment was wrong

I was covered in spray

It hadn't taken long

By the time I had finished

My effort was fair

The spray from the brush

Was everywhere!

I was literally covered

From head to toe

'You've got something in your hair mum

In case you didn't know!!'

So if I had to rate

The performance of the brush

I'd say take off your nightie

And don't do it in a rush

Someone more competent

Might fare better than me

I'm now having a lie down

And a nice cup of tea!!

The moral of the story

Is keep within your skill set

And employ a new cleaner

The best you can get

64 MY PARKINSON'S NURSE

I saw my Parkinson's nurse yesterday

As I haven't been feeling the best

Some things have been bothering me

That I needed to get off my chest

I haven't seen my neurologist

In a number of years

I don't feel I am missing out

My nurse allays all of my fears

We talked about my symptoms

And the things that I find tough

Then she explained the reasons

Why I'm feeling so rough

We looked for a solution

To some of my current woes

Like my resurfacing tremor

And my painfully curling toes

She asked about my habits

And how I sleep at night

THE GIFT

The pressures of my job

The balance of everything must be right

The answer to my problems

Is found in another pill

If I can stand the side affects

Which is purely down to will

I long for a solution

Relief of any kind

At least I can feel satisfied

It's not all in my mind

Parkinson's is relentless

It affects everything you do

It will only beat you if you let it

And I don't intend to!

Thank you to my Parkinson's nurse

You really are the best

Listening to me moan

And putting my mind at rest

65 BEHIND THE MASK

We're always being told

That we should be kind

But that is quite difficult

When you've things on you mind

The world is quite bleak

No one is aware

That you feel so sad

And you need them to care

Their lives go on

Nothing to hold them back

You sit on the sidelines

Aware of all that you lack

You aren't the person

People want to be around

OK at a distance

Is what I have found

I don't fit the demographic

Of somebody fun

So I decline invitations

It's better in the long-run

Or I don't get invited

People don't want me there

The misery who won't dance

What a waste of a chair

I don't want anyone's pity

Don't feel sorry for me

I won't ruin anyone's fun

But where does that leave me?

Parkinson's brings with it

Depression and anxiety

And with it, isolation

Who would want to be me?

This is not a pity party

This is just how I feel

Parkinson's awareness

Of the things we conceal

It upsets me sometimes

That I'm not good company

But I put on my mask

That's the me you all see

66 JUST FOR FUN!

Do you have a few drinks?

Or go out with friends?

Binge watch a whole series

To see how it ends?

Visit somewhere new?

A day out by the sea?

If you could choose anything

What would it be?

A spa day with your bestie?

A holiday abroad?

A walk in the countryside?

Whatever you can afford

Playing games on the console?

Or board games with the kids?

Shopping on eBay?

Keep raising your bids

Time spent with family

Every moment adored?

There is so much you can do

To stop you getting bored!

Throw a big party

Go to see a show

Spend the whole day shopping

Where will you go?

Time on your own

You can read a good book

Take photos, make memories

Ideas everywhere you look

Wherever you go

Whatever you do

Be spontaneous, unpredictable

Happiness will find you!

67 PROCRASTINATION

When you have something

You really don't want to do

You keep putting it off

Until you really have to

You'd rather do chores

Suddenly, you must clean the loo

That hair in the plug hole

Must be removed too

You've picked up the dog poo

The oven is clean

There isn't a dog hair

Anywhere to be seen

The bins have been emptied

The shopping is done

The washing is folded

This is almost fun!

You've spoken to friends

You've been meaning to call

And helped out a neighbour

No trouble at all!

But the thing you're avoiding

Still needs to be done

So little time left

Why haven't you begun?

Just get it over with

It won't be so bad

When it is done

You will feel glad

The deadline is looming

Panic is setting in

Why have you waited till now

To even begin?

Procrastination

Is another way to say

Putting off the inevitable

And wasting a day

68 CAKE

Read the recipe

You must get it right

Baking is a science

Your efforts will delight

Preheat the oven

Prepare your tin

Weigh the ingredients

Then you can begin

Butter and sugar

Eggs, you need four

Self-raising flour

To make a cake you adore

Beat them together

In a mixer or by hand

Add in some flavour

As the recipe demands

When it's well mixed

And smoothed into the tin

It's time for the oven

The baking can begin

You look through the glass

To watch as they rise

Golden in colour

Just like a sunrise

Out of the oven

Onto a cooling rack

If they haven't baked well

You can't put them back

The aroma of cake

Now fills the air

Your kids are lingering

Wondering whether you'll share

Finally cool

You can decorate your cake

It's surprising really

How much mess you can make

But when you are done

Everything clean and tidy

There's nothing nicer

Than cake for tea

69 THE DILEMMA

You have a dilemma

Weighing on your mind

You cannot decide

There's no answer to find

No right or wrong answer

It's up to you

You have a choice

What should you do?

You ask for opinions

And then don't agree

The only thing you can do

Is try it and see

Go with your gut

Will your heart rule your head?

Is it the end of he world

If you do that instead?

Don't be dissuaded

When you've made up your mind

The answer is out there

For you to find

Don’t ponder for too long

You’ll drive yourself mad

Weigh up your options

It won’t be so bad

Even wrong decisions

(Great in hindsight!)

Can often be rectified

Never give up the fight

70 PHOTOGRAPHING FRIENDS

I wanted a photo

Of my friends

Should be simple

But that really depends

Upon the friends

And on the day

There's no predicting

Either way

They won't want to be

In the photo at all

But you line them up

Beside the wall

Camera poised

Ignoring complaints

They misbehave

They are no saints!

Then composure restored

You take your shot

But the short one is squatting

And it all goes to pot!

If you are the shortest

You don't need to crouch

I got the top of your head

On that I can vouch

Then no one can pose

Or even stand still

Hilarity takes over

I'll get it, I will!

I finally get a photo

Three of them smile

Not perfect by far

But no filters for miles

My favourite people

Laughter and food

Time spent with them

Will always be good ♥

71 WAIT!

It took so long to accept you

When you entered my world

Denial, anger and frustration

Negativity unfurled

As time went by we reached a truce

Medication strengthened our bond

We muddled along together

Even becoming quite fond

I accepted your place in my life

Amused by things you made me do

You rewarded me with creativity

And instigated a poem or two

I realised I could live with you

As long as you knew your place

But just as we got comfortable

You showed a different face

I felt you had deceived me

But this was always your plan

Comfy for a little while

But things can't stay as they began

The medication doesn't work so well

I'm 'off' more than I'm 'on'

If I had to find someone to blame

You would be number one

Progressive doesn't mean much

Until it applies to you

When you notice you're getting worse

And wonder how much you can still do

You ramped up your game imperceptibly

I didn't realise what you'd done

Now my drugs aren't working so well

But don't think that you've won!

I'm doing my best to keep up with you

There are days when I cannot

Sometimes you overpower me

Everything goes to pot

I'm sure in time I will be back

Not quite where I was before

That's the nature of the beast

I'll never win this war

I only hope you're not in a rush

To reach the finish line

I cannot deny you your prize

I'm only asking for more time ...

72 METAPHORICALLY SPEAKING

Do you have a heart of stone

If you're unkind or cruel?

Are you nutty as a fruitcake

If you play the fool?

If you sleep peacefully in your bed

Do you sleep like a log?

If he is very, very happy

Are there two tails on your dog?

Are you the apple of my eye?

If I cherish you the most?

Is time really money?

Waste it at your cost!

Are you a couch potato?

If you watch a lot of telly?

If an idea stinks

It is bad rather than smelly

If you're the black sheep of the family

Are you really a disgrace?

If you are a hypocrite

Does that mean you're two-faced?

Can you actually fall in love?

Or be knocked off your feet?

Is the end always bitter?

And does success smell sweet?

73 THE WIND

A gentle breeze

On a hot summer's day

Cooling sun kissed cheeks

Blowing hair astray

Fluffy white clouds

Dance across the sky

Temporary relief

While the sun is so high

Stronger winds

Help to dry clean washing

Pegged on the line

Forever dancing

Forming a rainbow

As the wind lifts clothing high

They flap in the breeze

Very soon they'll be dry

Then there's the wind

You get before a storm

Blowing and howling

Stay indoors where it's warm!

It rattles your windows

And blows under your door

Blowing leaves off the trees

That then cover the floor

Damaging rooftops

And blowing down trees

It was so much nicer

When the wind was a breeze

We need the wind

To move the weather along

A nice, warm, gentle breeze

Nothing too strong!

74 BE KIND

Be kind in your heart

And all that you do

Then you will find

Others will be kind too

One tiny gesture

A few simple words

Could make a difference

Where kindness is inferred

Be there for others

Make time for friends

Smile… it's infectious!

We can make amends

Be loving and gracious

Listen more than you speak

Think what a difference

We could make in a week?!

If a week is too ambitious

Try it for one day

Keep kindness in your heart

And all that you say

A conscious effort

Is all that we need

For the world to be a kinder place

We can succeed

75 CELEBRATING MAY

Cherry blossom

On the tree

Such a delicate pink

For all to see

Apple blossom

Pure and white

In full bloom

Such a lovely sight

White and pink flowers

On the crab apple tree

Preceding the fruit

And looking so pretty

Laburnum flowers

Like golden yellow rain

Hanging from branches

Anything but plain

Little lambs tails

On a birch tree

Catkins appear first

Where nuts will eventually

The pussy willow

Furry and soft

Immediately recognised

Catkins held aloft

And then on the ground

Bluebells appear

Carpeting forest floors

With their fragrant beauty

Skies full of song

As the dawn chorus resumes

Nature's symphony

To match colourful spring blooms

76 INVISIBLE

Unseen

Unheard

Carry on

Undeterred

Undervalued

Unsatisfied

Silent tears

Presence denied

Unable

Misunderstood

Lost opportunities

I wish I could

Unknown

Unimportant

Eternally

Irrelevant

Uncertain

Unsure

Ignorance

You endure

Unlucky

Undone

Wishing you

Were not the one

Unequal

Unspoken

Eternally

Broken

Unnoticed

Unfit

Expectation

Get on with it!

77 WORTHLESS

What is your worth

To your family?

Are you loved

Unconditionally?

What is your worth

To your friends?

Do you share a bond

Which never ends?

What is your worth

To your workmates?

Do they support you?

Are they advocates?

What is your worth

To your spouse?

Are you soulmates?

Or do you just share a house?

What is your worth?

Do you hold any value?

Self-worth is essential

For you to be you!

78 THE CHOICE

Take it or leave it

It's up to you

No one else can choose

What you should do

Flip a coin

Heads or tails

Is it a choice

When luck prevails?

Ask a friend

What would they do?

Is their choice important?

They are not you

Go with your heart

Or go with your head

Sleep on a decision

When you go to bed

Do some research

Knowledge is key

What would you choose

If you were me?

79 FOREVER...

What does forever

Mean to you?

A relationship

Only for two

The home you create

For your family

Is this where

Your whole life will be?

A friendship bond

That cannot break

A career decision

Only you can make

Your role as a mother

Despite growing old

You'll always be there

As their lives unfold

Dedication as a grandparent

If you're lucky

Lessons from mistakes

Last an eternity

Promises made

To those who matter

A diagnosis

That causes your world to shatter

Memories you share

Never to fade

The person you are

Reputation made

Whoever you are

Whatever you do

Forever will hold

Different meaning for you

80 THE GARDEN

Bright sunshine

Blue sky

Birds tweeting

On the fly

Bees buzzing

Colourful blooms

The first roses

Delicate perfumes

Water dancing

In a fine spray

A water fountain

Droplets play

Butterflies pause

Nectar so sweet

A brief opportunity

For something to eat

Garden awakening

Buds wait to burst

Leaves unfurl

Which will come first?

Silence deafens

Broken by a chase

Dogs collapse exhausted

Can't keep up the pace!

81 BRITISH

There's nothing more British

Than a nice cup of tea

Or fish and chips

Eaten by the sea

Traditional Sunday dinner

Yorkshire pudding and roast beef

A full English breakfast

Great hangover relief

A red telephone box

A black taxi cab

Miserable weather

Makes everything drab

The Queen and her palaces

The Royal family

London and it's landmarks

It's the place to be!

Football and cricket

A nice pint of beer

Stonehenge and Shakespeare

Can all be found here

Confusing language

Accents extreme

Beautiful landscapes

Scones with clotted cream

I'm proud to be British

A Geordie to boot

No matter where life takes you

Remember your roots!

82 THE WORD GAME

A word game is tricky

To play every day

Against your mum

To win, come what May!

You take it in turns

To place words on the board

Eagerly anticipating

What you have scored

The aim of the game

Is to get the highest score

But my mum uses words

I've never heard of before

Combinations of letters

You're sure must be wrong

But your mum is insistent

And the game moves along

It's difficult to make words

From her gobbledygook

They're definitely not words

You'd find in a book!

But the game rages on

A tough battle is won

Quite a worthy winner

When all is said and done

I don't let her win

And she puts up a fight

Another game over

Until tomorrow night

83 DOG WALK LIMBO

Parkinson's means

I'm stiff and slow

So when I walk the dogs

I'm careful where I go

I walk on the flat

When there's no one about

I'm ever so choosy

About when I'll go out

This morning we went walking

Bright and early

Along the river

Just the dogs and me

A long walk

In the bright morning sun

Me and the dogs

That should be fun?!

It started off well

No one else was around

The ducks and the heron

The only sound

Then across our path

Was a fallen tree

There was no way around it

For the dogs and me

The tree itself

Left a gap underneath

No way I could crawl under

Even if I grit my teeth

Once on my knees

I'd never get up

Even with the help

Of a dog and a pup

I didn't want to go back

What else could I do?

I'm not your average person

So my choices were few

The gap under the tree

Came up to my neck

Surely I could just limbo?

Am I mad? What the heck?

Bending is a problem

I experience everyday

But limbo is different

Wouldn't you say?

As soon as I set off

I regretted my choice

Why on earth didn't I listen

To my inner voice?

A dog in each hand

Pulling me through

They're pulling too hard

Now what do I do?

I couldn't bend far enough

So I was caught on the tree

Who on earth thought limbo

Was an option for me?

Caught by the neck

On the branch of tree

Dragged by two dogs

I couldn't get free

Then dog number one

Spotted a squirrel up ahead

And yanked me off my feet

With no fear where he tread

No longer stuck

On the wrong side of the tree

Now sprawled on the path

Quite a sight to see!

I regained my composure

And checked we were alone

There were four golfers watching

I might've known!

So in future

Wherever I go

There's never a good reason

To attempt to limbo!!

84 BROWNIES

The boys wanted brownies

How could I resist?

Any excuse for baking

Oh if you insist!

My new ovens need testing

I need more practice you see

So what could be better

Than brownies for tea?

My last attempt failed

Quite miserably

Less brownie, more cake

How would this attempt be?

I followed the recipe

Topped with chopped chocolate bars

A Twirl and a Wispa

A Caramel and a Mars

Into the oven

I hardly dared look

Despite good intentions

It wasn't quite by the book

A bit of extra baking time

I had nothing to fear

Gooey chocolate brownies

Look how good they appear!

Taste test complete

They have passed the test

If you want brownies

Homemade are the best!!

85 A PARKINSON'S ALPHABET

P is for progressive

Parkinson's cannot be cured

A is for anxiety

Caused by all that you've endured

R is for rigidity

No longer able to bend

K is for kinesia

Brady is his friend

I is for insomnia

It's impossible to sleep

N is for neurologist

Appointments you should keep

S is for slowness

In everything you do

O is for overcoming challenges

You must face quite a few

N is for nerve cells

You are missing some

S is for stiffness

Hard to overcome

Parkinson's is the gift

That just keeps on giving

Just don't forget

That life is for living!

86 SLEEP

Don't wake me if I'm sleeping

Sleep evades me at every turn

Don't disturb me if I'm snoring

It's not a difficult lesson to learn

If I take all of the duvet

Or more than my share of the bed

Don't wake me from my slumber

Or try to reduce my spread

Ignore me when I'm drooling

Or my hair is in your face

I'm shouting in my dreams

Or acting out a race

At least during those moments

I'm actually fast asleep

Let's face it, there won't be many nights

Where I don't make a peep

I can't lie still for long

I toss and turn all night

Until I get stuck in the bed

Not a pretty sight!

I'd manage life so much better

With a good night's sleep

But that is such a rarity

Good sleep does not come cheap

I'd sacrifice so many things

For a decent rest

But if a few hours is the most I'll get

I'll settle for second best!

87 DON'T GO OUT IN THE DARK WITH YOUR SOCKS ON

It's never a good idea

Even if it's just for a second

Things are never as they appear

Don't go out in the dark with your socks on

You'll regret it if you do

At least put on your slippers

It only takes a moment or two

Don't go out in the dark with your socks on

Turn on a torch or a light

You don't know what could be lurking

Out there in the dead of night

I went out in the dark with my socks on

So the dog could have a wee

I stood on a slug which squelched underfoot

So now I feel sick, naturally!

88 THE INTERVIEW

My husband Mark, works from home

He's quite high up in IT

Sometimes working from a home office

Is not an ideal place to be

Today he's conducting interviews

Via a video call

With me and the dogs in the house

Interruptions not tolerated at all

It was all going rather well

The dogs were behaving too

So I decided to make a coffee

Mark said I could take his through

As long as I couldn't be seen on camera

So 'stealth mode' it would be

I crept in and left his coffee

Confident no one had seen me

Apparently I don't do 'stealth mode'

On camera for all to see

Me in my Oodie and PJs

Tiptoeing in with a cup of coffee

There followed an awkward silence

No one knew what to say

I'd interrupted the interview

In quite a spectacular way

Stealth is not in my skill set

I'm not sure why I thought it would be?!

Just carrying something and walking

Is quite a challenge for me!

Apologies to Thomas

You looked like a nice chap

I hope your interview went well

Despite my little mishap

I feel I must blame my hubby

He must take some responsibility

For telling me I could take him his coffee

And having the camera pointing at me!

89 POOPER SCOOPER

One of the most tedious jobs

Is picking up poo

But when you have a dog

It's something you must do

It's amazing to think

How many times

You pick up poo

Within a lifetime

Factor in

An inability to bend

And if you try

You come to a sticky end

So a solution

You have to find

For this yucky problem

Bearing in mind

Your disabilities

And particular needs

But with the help of Google

You finally succeed

And buy a Pooper Scooper

So great, you're in awe

You've never seen one

Like this before

A Pooper Scooper

Of such enormous size

You'll never have a problem

Bagging your prize

But a problem arose

You did not foresee

The poo bags you had

We're far too tiny

So before you could try it

You had to wait

But it was worth it

For a Pooper Scooper this great!

90 PAIN

Subjective at best

The threshold is unique

Whatever the cause

Relief you must seek

A constant companion

No chance of a cure

Your strength will determine

Your will to endure

Do you give up?

Give in to the pain?

Let it dictate

Drive you insane?

Or do you fight back?

And push the pain aside

Doing your best

Some things you can't hide

Pain brings misery

If you let it win

People will judge

Much to your chagrin

Pain is a challenge

It puts you to the test

As long as people know

You are doing your best

Walk a mile in my shoes

Imagine pain every day

There's nothing you can do

To make it go away

Pain is my norm

My unwelcome friend

My constant bedfellow

With me to the end

91 I HAVE A NAME

Don't call me 'Babe'

Or 'Princess' or 'Pet'

I'm not your 'Angel'

I've a name, don't forget!

I'm not your 'Love'

'Hun' or 'Sweetheart'

And as for 'Duck'

Where do I start?

I'm definitely not a 'Precious'

I'm not a 'Sweetie' or a 'Dear'

If you call me 'Darling'

You would get a thick ear

These pet names are something

Life partners would share

But if you don't know me

My name is Clare!

92 PAWS IN THE PARK

Is the place to be

If you're a canine

Who likes to run free

An hour with your friends

Will wear you out

Running and chasing

Around and about

Two middle aged women

Supply balls and treats

They don't move far

Luckily there are seats

There's agility equipment

But we're not keen

And through a gate

There's even a stream

But we are happy

Just running around

And when we're sick of photos

There are poos to be found

We keep the women busy

When they've sat for too long

They think they've worn us out

So we prove them wrong

Then battle commences

We're not keen to leave

Dogs to get in cars

And balls to retrieve

We say our goodbyes

To Paws in the Park

We'll be back again

To play and to bark (eh Bruce?!)

93 STUCK

It's difficult to describe

How it feels to be 'stuck'

You just cannot move

You have run out of luck

Today on our walk

Just the dogs and me

In the beautiful sunshine

Along the river, us three

We walked and we walked

In the warmth of the sun

As we reached the river

The real walk had just begun

We carried on along the river

To a particular tree

Where river access was easy

Not for the dogs, for me!

It was probably too far

I'm not great at exercise

Well if I'm honest

It's one thing I despise

But we made it and we paddled

The dogs had so much fun

But little did I realise

The real fun had just begun

Miles from home

And without any warning

I was stuck

And the truth was slowly dawning

In the middle of nowhere

Just the dogs and me

No one for miles

Just an occasional tree

I had my phone

I could call Mark

But he was in a meeting

I'd have to wait until it was dark!

The dogs chose that moment

To go completely crazy

Running round in circles

Their leads wrapped around me

Two wet dogs

Trying to get to one another

Who's bright idea was this?

I'm never having another

Then at that precise moment

I swallowed a fly

Coughing and choking

I thought I might die!

I did have some foresight

I'd brought water with me

A quick drink would do it

The bottle was soon empty

Coughing and spluttering

And red in the face

Sweat pouring from me

I looked a disgrace

Eventually I managed

To untangle each hound

Before I completely unbalanced

And fell to the ground

At that point I realised

I just couldn't move

Parkinson's had played a trump card

And was just getting in his groove

My right leg was useless

A dead weight at best

How would I get home?

This would be quite a test

Somehow we managed

To get moving again

What should take a minute

Was taking ten

The pain was unreal

I tried not to pout

Just in case, by some fluke

There were people about

Definitely not people

This surely could not be

A herd of cows

Blocking the gate from me!

We made very slow progress

I hoped they would depart

They had no intention

Of moving apart

They just lay there mooing

And chewing the cud

I didn't know what to do

Or even if I could

While I was debating

What I should do

I turned to find Bruce

Eating cow poo

Surely my day

Couldn't get any worse

Despite being blessed

With the Parkinson's curse

I'll end it now

This tale of woe

Next time anyone suggests a walk

I probably shouldn't go!

94 MY WISH FOR YOU

Hope for the hopeless

We can always choose hope

Calm for the frantic

It helps us to cope

Luck for the unlucky

We all deserve a chance

Action for the inactive

Allow your spirit to dance

Wisdom for the ignorant

Knowledge is everything

Success for the unsuccessful

And all that it can bring

Peace for the conflicted

Your heart must be happy

Healing for the sick

Good health is everything to me

Love for the unloved

Everyone deserves this

Happiness for the sad

Just a little can be bliss

Justice for the wronged

We should live by our virtues

Kindness for the unkind

Walk a mile in my shoes

Quiet for the noisy

To give you time to think

Generosity for the poor

We must help those on the brink

Friendship for the lonely

Such a difference it can make

Security for the insecure

Not everyone is fake

Time for the rushed

Important things can pass you by

Determination for the defeated

It never hurts to try

95 CONTENTMENT

Contentment in life

Is what we aim for

It doesn't relate

To being rich or poor

It's not about status

Or material things

How big your house is

Living like kings

Contentment is family

It's what makes you happy

Doing things you love

Spending time cos it's free

Living your life

With people who care

Appreciating every moment

Feelings laid bare

Generosity of spirit

Kindness in your heart

Little things mean a lot

It’s what sets us apart

Strive for contentment

In all that you do

Don’t waste your life

Wishing for something new

Have peace in your heart

Accept your lot

Be grateful for opportunities

And all that you’ve got

96 I MISS YOU

Fleetingly

You catch my eye

But when I look

You're camera shy

A gentle breeze

A cool reprieve

I'm sure you were here

Why did you leave?

Shadows dapple

Obscure the view

In the distance

Is that you?

Imprinted memories

Trick my mind

Leaving clues

For me to find

No matter what

I feel you near

Your voice whispers

For me to hear

Whether imagined

Or whether it's true

I'll spend my days

Remembering you

97 SPEAK ENGLISH!

I'm definitely not vibing

I don't know what that means

This is my life now

With a house full of teens

They speak a different language

I need a phrase book

Would you say I'm thicc?

You just need to look

Apparently I'm a boomer

But I don't have a clue

I don't know what wag wan means

What's up with you?

I'm definitely not poggers

Or even just pog

No wonder I spend

So much time with the dog!

I'm not a Karen

I'm not in a ship

I don’t have a bruh

Don’t describe me as drip

I don’t understand

Most things that they say

But perhaps it is best

If it remains that way!

They think I’m embarrassing

I probably am

But I’m not salty

I still have my fam!

98 THE ROSE

Exquisite petals

Gently unfurled

Pastel perfection

Scent out of this world

Time spent in bud

An eternity

Releasing a bloom

Of unequalled beauty

Thorny protection

On robust stems

A prickly perennial

Delicately condemns

Year after year

Flawless flora persist

A tender memorial

How much you are missed

99 WHAT ARE WE TEACHING OUR CHILDREN?

Incy Wincy Spider

Catching all the flies

I just walked through your web

It caught me by surprise

Humpty Dumpty on that wall

You should take more care

The resources you use when you fall

Are more than your fair share!

Twinkle, twinkle little star

Up there in the sky

Of course we know what you are

That you can't deny!

Old McDonald had a farm

With cows and pigs and sheep

Ducks and chickens and a horse

When did he find time to sleep?!

Sing a song of twenty quid

Sixpence is not legal tender

As for black birds in a pie

Not a great contender!

Hey diddle diddle

There's no cat and no fiddle

Cows are not jumping over the moon

I'd be worried if they were

Life is not a cartoon

100 BEAUTIFUL RAIN

Heavy grey clouds

Saturate the sky

Depressing the sunlight

Raindrops testify

Cumulonimbus

Distort the sun

Precipitation

Drops fall one by one

Comfortingly melodious

Droplets strike the ground

Distinctive pitter patter

Such a familiar sound

Refreshingly reassuring

Rainfall on your skin

Dancing in the rain

And puddle-jumping

Fresh earthy scents

After a downpour

As the clouds break

You're hoping for more

And then as the sun's rays

Mix with drops of rain

A wonderful arc of colour

Is all that remains

A meteorological phenomenon

Refraction of light

In tiny raindrops

What a beautiful sight

101 HOMOPHONES

Those four cakes are for you

You ate them at eight o'clock?

Were you bored looking at the board?

You need to sew the whole hole in your sock

Did you hear the tale about the dog with two tails?

You can bring two friends to tea too

Did you see the sea on your holiday?

When I sit here I can't hear you

Has your aunt got rid of that ant's nest?

Will we be able to see some bees?

I spy with my little eye

I know there are no leaves on the trees

Their friends are waiting over there

My son says the sun makes him feel happy

Don't whine because you can't have any wine

By the way, you are buying our tea!

Did you break the brake on your bicycle?

It would be great if you could grate some cheese?

Did you catch sight of our new website?

We'll need an hour for our meeting please

102 ORNITHOPHOBIA

This morning a bird woke me

Tapping on the window

What on earth did he want?

I really didn't want to know

He wasn't just a little bird

The sight filled me with fear

So I shouted to my husband

Who made the bird disappear

That wasn't good enough for me

I had to know the bird had gone

So I ventured into the garden

With my nightie on

I couldn't see it anywhere

With relief I went inside

But as I made a cup of tea

I thought of places it might hide

I'd hardly finished making a brew

When the tapping recommenced

This time not on the window

But a mirror I'd leaned on the fence

Jeered on by two mates squawking

The bird was giving it some force

I worried the mirror might break

Or fall and squash the bird, of course

The dogs refused to go outside

While the bird continued its attack

It was fighting its own reflection

But nothing was fighting back

My anxiety was rising

What was I to do?

I needed to go out into the garden

To pick up the dog poo

I decided I needed a photo

And ventured outside

Apparently my presence was enough

For the performance to subside

The squawking from the rooftop

Frantically got louder still

Urging their mate to get out of there

I didn't really wish him any ill

So I didn't get a photograph

The birds are now long gone

My anxiety is subsiding

But I wonder for how long??

103 THE CAROUSEL HORSE

Frozen mid gallop

For an eternity

A circular steeplechase

It will never be free

The carousel horse

Destined to life in one place

Festooned in bright colours

A painted smile on its face

My horse is different

It's happy and free

Depicting NHS heroes

And words from my poetry

Overlooking the church

And the river below

Such a peaceful location

He's happy, you know

The rest of the horses

Are dotted about

All over town

You must seek them out

A whole carousel of horses

Each one unique

Representing our lives

There are 30 to seek

There’s no eerie music

Of the calliope

Just beautiful horses

Each where it should be

104 THE BEACH

Crashing waves

Dance across wet sand

Circling seagulls

Not daring to land

Thundery skies

Threaten to break

Moved by howling gales

Realise their mistake

Rays of sunshine

Pierce the cloud

Illuminating beach huts

Standing tall and proud

A solitary figure

Punctuates the scene

Footprints in the sand

Where has he been?

Pebbles and shells

Offered by the sea

Left by the tide

A memento for me...?

The tide surges on

Endeavours to reach land

Swirling white foam

Advances across the sand

Evidence of creatures

Who inhabit the sea

Left on the beach

Amongst the other debris

105 THE MENOPAUSE

Menopause symptoms

Are not much fun

But in reality

The fun's just begun

The treatment prescribed

Is patches for me

What I'd prefer

Is a miracle really

I take out a patch

Anticipating great stuff

I read the instructions

Expectations enough

I read them again

As questions arise

It seems relatively simple

To my surprise

Let's get on with it

There's nothing to lose

But my tired brain

Is easy to confuse

Stick on a patch

Below the waist

You cannot restick it

So don't apply in haste

There was my error

The damage was done

I stuck it on my thigh

And then moved it to my bum

It didn't really seem to stick

So I pressed it firmly

Not entirely convinced

It was where it should be

Nothing much happened

I checked it each day

I'd expected great things

Much to my dismay

Had I stuck on the patch

Or the backing bit?

Nothing would surprise me

I'm a bit of a half-wit!

When it came to replace it

Three days had gone by

But could I find it

On my bum or my thigh?!

Panic set in

Where could it be?

As I'd placed it behind me

I couldn't see

What if the dog found it

What would it do?

It's too late now

On went patch number two

I'm a bit of a cynic

Not convinced it will work

And in the meantime

The dog's gone beserk!

106 MY HAPPY PLACE

The warmth of the sun

As it falls upon my face

And the sound of the waves

Make this my happy place

We don’t mind the weather

As we walk with heads bent

Looking for treasure

Many hours we have spent

A greeny blue shard

Hidden in plain sight

Insignificant to most

They don’t share your delight

A moment to ponder

And take in the view

Content to just be

For a minute or two

The squawk of a seagull

And a meteorological shift

The turning of the tide

Debris starts to drift

The feeling of sand

Cold and wet beneath my feet

The tide marches on

And we admit defeat

Happy to move inland

Chased by the sea breeze

Eating chips from the paper

Greedy gulls don't say 'please'

Time to go home

But we'll be back again

To my happy place

I just don't know when

107 WHEN ONE DOOR CLOSES

It's not the end

Just a reminder

There's more round the bend

The end of one chapter

Does not mean full stop

It's a chance to reflect

On all that you've got

Choose where you go

And what you do

Happiness is a priority

So you do you!

Don't compare your life

No two are the same

Enjoy every moment

There's no one to blame

Wherever life takes you

Do whatever you must

To make you happy

With people you trust

Life is for living

Don't forget that

However you do it

Wherever you're at

Success is measured

By reaching your goal

As long as that makes you happy

In your heart and soul

When one door closes

That one might be shut

But another will open

To get you out of that rut

108 SHREDDED

Bags of paperwork

Kept for years

Boxes of schoolbooks

Memories induce tears

Letters written

In a time gone by

Photos for passports

Ready to fly

Pictures drawn

In childish hand

Manuals for appliances

No longer in demand

School reports

Document each child

Letters from school

When they've gone wild

Details of pets

Houses from the past

Paper shredded

But memories last

109 US

Me and you

You and me

Together forever

For eternity

Muddling along

Doing our thing

Our little family

Is everything

Living our lives

Doing good stuff

Feeling content

We are enough

Facing challenges

Together as one

Celebrating together

Challenges won

We have each other

That's all we need

If we are happy

We can succeed

Wealth isn't important

You need somebody there

To share in your life

And to love and care

Someone to talk to

To share good times and bad

Someone to make memories

Oh the adventures you've had!

Who else would come out

In the middle of the night?

So I can take photographs

It must've been quite a sight!

But there you were

Always by my side

Every crazy idea

You support, terrified!

But I got my photo

I’m crazy, it’s true!

All thanks to my soulmate

Where would I be without you?!

110 THE KISS

A peck on the cheek

Or a smacker on the lips

A full blown kiss

While he's holding your hips

A kiss for hello

And a kiss for goodbye

A kiss when you're happy

A kiss when you cry

A teasing kiss

How far will you go?

A sloppy, wet kiss

From a child on tiptoe

The thrill of a kiss

When you get down and dirty

Stealing a kiss

When you're feeling flirty

Blowing a kiss

A kiss on the forehead

A goodnight kiss

When you go to bed

Perhaps a French kiss?

Kissing your earlobe and neck

A slow passionate kiss

Or maybe just a quick peck

Kissing is something

Everyone does

It releases dopamine

And gives you a loving buzz

111 STRONGER TOGETHER

Whether at work

Or whether at home

Teamwork is the answer

Don't do things alone

Involve your colleagues

There is no I in team

Sharing ideas

Is easier than it seems

Encouraging others

To play a part

Learning to listen

It's quite an art

Overcoming biases

For equality

Embracing differences

And diversity

Inclusion is easy

Treat everyone the same

We're stronger together

Teamwork is the aim

With that in mind

There are things we must do

To be stronger together

And that includes you!

Changes need action

It will take more than just me

But if we all work together

How great we could be!

112 THE MOAN

We moan about the heat

Mind it was very hot!

Then we moan about cloud

When the rain's all we've got

We moan about noise

When we're in bed

We moan about other people

The things that they've said

We moan when we're invited

Somewhere we don't want to go

Or if it's with people

We don't really know

We moan about kids

Disturbing our peace

We moan about money

Prices on the increase

We moan when it's busy

And we've got stuff to do

We moan when you don't help

But we've not asked you to

We moan about work

When it's too late to act

We moan about everything

After the fact

We moan about night

We moan about day

We moan about anything

Even when we're okay

We moan to our partners

Who pretend to hear

Until you ask them a question

Which is their biggest fear!

We moan about life

As it's passing us by

Missed opportunities

Stop moaning, just try!

113 WHO AM I?

The person you see

Looking back at you

When you look in the mirror

Is your reflection true?

The 'you' you imagine

Yourself to be

Is that the same 'you'

Other people see?

The 'you' as a wife

The 'you' your husband adores

The 'you' as a mum

The 'you' your kids ignore

The 'you' on holiday

Relaxing at last

The 'you' with family

Haunted by your past

The 'you' at the shops

The 'you' doing chores

The 'you' walking the dog

The 'you' who lives next door

The 'you' at work

That your colleagues know

The 'you' with friends

Does the true 'you' ever show?

So many versions

Of a person you see

But you get to choose

Which you to be

114 THE EVENING SKY

The evening sky

Is my favourite thing

Stunning sunsets

Birds on the wing

Fluffy white clouds

Bearing a pink hue

Contrails dissect

Where there are a few

Are they coming or going?

We'll never know

As the trail disappears

Into the bright orange glow

As day turns to night

There's a bright crescent moon

Illuminating the sky

Until clouds repugn

And then in the distance

Before the light disappears

A dragon-shaped cloud

Momentarily appears

A sky full of stars

Clouds hide it above

But I've had my moment

The evening sky I love

115 THE PATH THROUGHT THE WOODS

There's a path through the woods

You don't know where it goes

As you peer through the trees

It's where dappled sunlight shows

There's a path through the woods

You've not seen it before

Its beauty draws you in

Should you follow it some more?

There's a path through the woods

That leads you astray

A gentle breeze disturbs the canopy

Beckoning you that way

There's a path through the woods

It's off the beaten track

You must reach the natural end

Before you can turn back

There's a path through the woods

It's not a secret any more

Our favourite place to watch

Sunset from the shore

116 SEASIDE SELF-CARE

The very best self care

Is achieved by the sea

The bracing sea air

And the tranquillity

The wind in your face

And sand between your toes

At the sound of the waves

The pace of life slows

You sit on soft sand

As the sun warms your face

And paddle in clear water

Until waves begin to chase

You search amongst pebbles

For a souvenir

Something to take home

To remind you, you were here

To remind you to pause

To do what you need to do

Whatever it takes

To find the old you

You're in their somewhere

At times we can see

Like sea glass in the sand

This is where you should be

Little colourful glimpses

Waiting to be found

Put them altogether

Eternally bound

Beautiful sea glass

Tiny treasures for me

To remind me of this moment

I am where I should be

117 A GEORDIE LASS AT HEART!

A reet canny lass

Took us in her car

Aal the wa' tiv Newcassel

It was canny far

I was gannin up north

Tiv see me mutha

Thor wasn't time

Tiv see me brother

We went doon tiv Warkworth

Tiv gan in the sea

It was geet canny

But we went hyem for tea

We were gannin doon toon

For a deek and some scran

When a gadgie bumped into us

And a said, 'Howay man!'

He said, 'Y'alreet pet?!'

But a never sed nowt

He was a workyticket

And might give us a clout!

Toon was geet busee

At the sunda' market

So we went for some scran

While bairns cried for kets

The charvas were oot

Wearing nae clobber

Wuh had a canny laugh

Cos wuh weor dressed propa

Aa'd a deed canny time

It was ower an' aaal fast

A Geordie at heart

Aa've had a blast!

118 THE MOON

Your brilliant white light

Illuminates the night sky

So different to the sun

But you don't need to try

A perfect outline

Against an inky black night

A smattering of stars

You remain the highlight

The same familiar face

Beaming down from above

As you watch us sleeping

A symbol of love

So many iterations

Each one dependent on the sun

How much is reflected

Is what you become

The infamous crescent moon

From childhood story books

To the glorious super moon

I never tire of how it looks

119 HOT!

I’m boiling

It’s sweltering

It’s terribly hot

I’m sweating

I’m melting

I kid you not!

It’s scorching

It’s tropical

I’m red in the face

It’s roasting

I’m burning

Please, no warm embrace!

A heatwave

It’s muggy

I’m perspiring a lot

Balmy summer

Bright sunshine

Did I mention, it’s hot?!

120 THE JOURNEY

Life is a journey

Destination unknown

Sometimes with others

Often alone

Each journey is different

Some fast and some slow

Some go past familiar scenery

Some never know

Sometimes it is peaceful

You have chance to rest

Sometimes it is rough

Every turn is a test

Sometimes it is joyful

You want it to last

That's the thing about journeys

They're over too fast

My journey is rough

I feel every bump

I long for a smooth path

With just the odd hump

The odd twist or turn

I'd expect on my way

Not a road full of bumps

Every single day!

A straight path would bore me

It wouldn't be fun

To just keep on going

Eternally overdone

Every single journey

Ends the same way

You just don't know the destination

And you don't know the day

121 THINK OF ME

Think of me when you waken

The sunrise as bright as my smile

Think of me in the dawn chorus

The birdsong makes you pause for a while

Think of me in the fluffy clouds

Forming familiar shapes in the sky

Think of me in the raindrops

Like tears falling from your eye

Think of me in the rainbow

A sign that I'm still near

Think of me in the breeze

And the whispers you can hear

Think of me in the sunbeam

And the warmth you feel on your skin

Think of me in the reflection

And the feeling you get within

Think of me in the music

Emotions running free

Think of me in the perfume

The scent unique to me

Think of me in the photograph

Memories so true

Think of me in the darkness

And know I’m thinking of you

122 THE (NOT SO) LITTLE WALK!

Mark and I have a habit

Of doing crazy stuff

So last night we decided

The Royal Albert Hall wasn't enough

So at 10 o'clock at night

We thought we'd go for a stroll

Buckingham Palace didn't look far

So that was our goal

We set off at a pace

Marvelling at the sights

Working out what they were

Caused one or two fights!

As we trudged on

We soon had a thought

It was taking much longer

Than we thought it ought

We consulted Google maps

And the truth became clear

It was actual MILES

And I don't walk far, my dear!

But we were already out

And we'd seen many a thing

So we carried on

To the home of our King

Past Harrods and Harvey Nicks

Hyde Park and the Wellington Arch

Walking in the footsteps

Of last week's funeral march

We marvelled at the flames

On the Commonwealth Gates

And walked down Constitution Hill

As the peace resonates

We reached Buckingham Palace

And paid our respects

Others were doing the same

The solemnity reflects

We took a quick photo

To prove that we'd been

But it's not the same

Now there isn't a Queen

Suddenly realisation dawns

Of the physical abilities we lack

The hotel is miles away

And now we've got to get back!

123 THE TRAIN JOURNEY

The tinny cacophony of someone's too-loud music

Accompanies the hum of the train on the track

We progress on our journey, destinations unknown

As the doors slide shut and there's no going back

All walks of life represented within

Reside upon green upholstery unloved and worn

The sway of the train rocking passengers as one

As we snake through the countryside, dissecting fields of corn

The repetitive directive of 'tickets please?!'

Punctuates the air, distinct of the hum of meaningless chatter

Rustling through luggage, searching for necessary documents

We pull into a station and doors open with a clatter

Onward we go gaining disgruntled travellers

Shoving and pushing to reach empty seats

Claiming their prize with a backpack or suitcase

At every station this ritual repeats

Eventually our destination is the next to be reached

We wobble unsteadily to the nearest door

Minding the gap as instructed by faceless voices

We jump to the safety of the platform floor

Announcements are made and doors clatter shut

Travellers curse as the train leaves them behind

We stand in the sunshine awaiting our connection

Fortunately for us this journey has been kind

124 AUTUMN

Crisp notes in the air

As the day fades to night

The beginnings of frost

At the first morning light

The leaves on the trees

Orange, yellow, red and gold

Dark nights creep in

As autumn unfolds

Conkers and acorns

Berries in abundance

Crimson red toadstool caps

Bats full of romance

Birds on the wing

Migration their goal

The earth breathes a sigh

Summer has taken its toll

It's time for hibernation

Warm cosy nights in

Time for woolly jumpers

Let autumn begin

125 SPAGHETTI JUNCTION HATRED

Lights flicker in the dark

Vehicles swerve into place

Overhead directions flash

No one can win this race

Crimson brake lights illuminate

Mistakes recognised too late

Alternatives don't satisfy

Spaghetti junction hate

Chances taken as tempers rise

Gestures unnoticed in the night

Road rage wasted energy

Hope flickers like the light

Directions seem illogical

Override them at your peril

Headlights illuminate your space

Some drivers are feral

Finally you're on your way

Your nemesis navigated

Your son is back at university

Spaghetti junction hatred

126 LOVE IS...

Letting you sleep

Knowing you get little rest

That first cup of tea

Is always the best

Putting on the heating

Just as you wake up

The warm slice of toast

Left beside your cup

Doing the housework

So you don't have to

Making you laugh

When you're feeling blue

Sharing a sweet

Or the last piece of cake

Planning a holiday

Or a trip you'll both take

Walking the dog

When your joints cause you pain

Cooking anything you fancy

Because you're nauseous again

Watching bad TV

Because it makes you smile

Going on a date

It has been a while

A lingering hug

After a hard day

A moment of shared silence

There's nothing to say

Collecting prescriptions

So your meds don't run out

This is our reality

This is what love is about

127 COLD

It's freezing

It's chilly

It's bitter today

It's biting

It's nippy

It's arctic you'd say

It's glacial

It's parky

It's polar out there

It's snowy

It's Baltic

Brass monkeys beware

It's frosty

It's icy

You feel shivery

It's bracing

I'm frozen

Cos it's cold, you see!

128 MY LOVELY MOON

Steadfast and eternal

Reflections of sunlight

A soft milky glow

In the inky black night

A monochrome sky

Punctuated by starlight

Waxing and waning

She rules the night

Moonbeams kiss the earth

With whispers of light

Pathways to the heavens

As your dreams take flight

The moon has your heart

Guiding you with her light

So she can be seen

She must dwell in the night

129 THE VIEW THROUGH MY WINDOW

Spattered with enduring raindrops

And the lingering cold grime of life

Evading the efforts of a persistent sun

Behind it, a man and his wife

Hindered by brickwork and metal

Dampened by the dullness of life

A hint of the beauty of nature

Entwined in harsh grey by the wife

Memories held in reflection

A rainbow arcs high in cloudy skies

The man and his wife have been happy here

Their truth is a glint in sapient eyes

The wife cleans the grime from the window

Pirouetting sunbeams reflected in the glass

The husband softly kisses the wife on the cheek

Knowing rain clouds eventually pass

The view hasn't changed much in ten years

The man and his wife doggedly content

Determined to create the best view

When life obstinately refuses to relent

The glass in the window is fragile

Reflecting the life contained within

Weakness causes the glass to break

And the view of their lives therein

130 WHISPERS ON THE WIND

Can you hear the whispers

Carried on the wind?

Voices of the faceless

Unjustly chagrined

Eternal susurration

An hypnotic cacophony

Quietly emotive

The sonance of the free

Can you hear the whispers

Of an imperceptible evangelist?

Surreptitious murmurings

Ominously missed

Momentary quietude

As the breeze subsides

Concealed by the Doldrums

The whispering decides

Can you hear the whispers

Calling out your name?

THE GIFT

Softly from inky shadows

The wind is not to blame

Hushed asseverations

Onerous to perceive

Whispers on the wind

Discernible if you believe

131 WHAT DO I WANT YOU TO KNOW?

I want you to know that I'm trying

When my body fails me

I know how funny it must look

But this is not how I chose to be

I want you to know that I'm tired

Tired of doing this every day

Tired of the pills and the symptoms

Tired of the things people say

I want you to know that I'm frightened

I worry about not being enough

I don't want to be a burden

When progression means things will get tough

I want you to know I'm still in here

The person you knew before

Before Parkinson's changed everything

Striving to even the score

I want you to know I'm determined

To be the best me that I can

Some days are easier than others

Impossible to predict or to plan

I want you to know I'm resilient

Parkinson's won't beat me

The future for me is uncertain

I can't give in, you see?!

I want you to know that I'm hopeful

I don't want to give up yet

Hope gives me reason to smile every day

When hope is the best you can get

I want you to know that I'm happy

Despite all the challenges ahead

I have so much to be grateful for

Like the wonderful man that I wed

My children are my inspiration

My dog makes me smile every day

My mum gives me strength in abundance

I'm doing Parkinson's my own way!

132 MORNING HAS BROKEN

In the gentle hush of the morning

When the world is yet to wake

The sun hesitates on the horizon

As the dawn begins to break

The birds withhold their chorus

There's a damp chill in the air

The world pauses for a moment

A sense of peace everywhere

Subdued by a deafening silence

As you anticipate the day ahead

A moment of calm reflection

To steady the thoughts in your head

Some gentle affirmations

As the world begins to stir

This moment will be lost soon

As life takes on a chaotic blur

You notice the first rays of sunlight

Birdsong heralds a new day

You embrace the person you can be

In life's delicate interplay

133 THE MIDWIFE

Behind the tiredness

I still see a smile

A hint of your passion

Hidden for a while

Behind the frustration

I still see the care

The heartfelt compassion

That's always been there

Behind the hustle and bustle

I still see you

Devoted and resilient

In all that you do

Behind the silence

I still hear your voice

Striving for change

Whilst still offering choice

Behind the media headlines

I see broken hearts

Midwives doing their best

Despite those news reports

Behind it all

I see a person, that's you!

People are quick to forget

Midwives are people too!

134 THE CROW

A curious fellow

Proclaiming his intent

Loud and mercurial

Of choleric temperament

Dishevelled presentation

Narrative unknown

Furtive in his manner

Operating alone

Committed endeavour

Determined pursuit

A beak full of peanuts

His bountiful loot

135 THE POET

Always a poet

Even in prose

Reflections on life

Blessings and woes

Moments in time

Depicted in verse

Imperfect perceptions

Life does not rehearse

Emotive sentiments

Chronicled poesy

Choreograph jumbled thoughts

Into poetry

ABOUT THE AUTHOR

Clare was diagnosed with Parkinson's Disease in 2018 and believes that her diagnosis also brought with it the gift of creativity. This is her third and biggest poetry collection and is inspired by the love and support of all of the important people in her life. This book represents Clare's gift to you as her way of saying thank you.

Printed in Great Britain
by Amazon

33864237R00175